"Most people know they are created for something greater or that they can accomplish more of the things that are important to them. Few know how to make it happen. *Move! You're in Your Own Way* provides techniques to unlock personal possibilities with clear steps for making their desires real."

— **Edwina Martin Arnold,** *author of Chocolate Friday*

"This book is refreshing and a must add to any collection of self-help books you may have. It will add value and insight in areas of your life that you have dreamed of."

— **Saba Tekle,** *Publisher, Mentor and best-selling author of 20 Beautiful Women*

In *Move! You're In Your Own Way,* author Patricia Knight has turned over every stone and identified every potential obstacle or possible argument that you could use to keep playing small in your life. With clarity, humor, plenty of real life examples, inspiring quotes, and a rich collection of simple but powerful exercises, this book is a must-read self-coaching guide to creating an extraordinary life you love!"

—**Debrena Jackson Gandy,** *national best-selling Author, Speaker, Mentor and Success Coach*

A Note From The Author

The image on the book is a peek into a kaleidoscope with many colored glass pieces.

When I was a kid I loved kaleidoscopes. When you first look into it the pieces of glass form a beautiful image. And when you turned it even a little, the exact same pieces shifted and formed a brand new beautiful image.

When you are able to shift even a small aspect of yourself, your perception changes, and the shift opens up new poss-ibilities for your life.

You have all the pieces needed to make things happen. To gain greater satisfaction in your life, make a slight shift.

Move! You're in Your Own Way

7 Steps to Designing an Extraordinary Life

Patricia Knight

Foreword by

National Best Selling Author Debrena Jackson Gandy

7 Publishing

Seattle, Washington

DEDICATION

This book is dedicated to my greatest gifts; Melany, Justin, Yasmin, Taylor and PJ.

You are the loves of my life and the continual source of my joy and pride.

ACKNOWLEDGEMENTS

I am eternally grateful for the people in my life.

My greatest blessings are my family, Melany Willis, Justin Cook, Yasmin Fuller, Taylor Fuller and PJ Fuller. They are my cheering squad and are always there for me. They encourage and believe in me. And I adore them all.

My incredible friends Michelle Fulbright and Rhonda Salverson applaud every step I take. Their support has helped me in many aspects of my life.

My publisher Saba Tekle who advised me on the many details that took my book from manuscript to reality.

My writers group Edwina Martin Arnold, Mary Mitchell, Vanessa McClendon, and Crystal Shaw: They read, reviewed and gave input on multiple drafts.

My clients who first said, "Are the concepts you teach written down?" (Now they are!) Coaching them has been an education and opportunity for both of us to grow.

There are many incredible authors and speakers whose work helped shape my life and inspired me to strive for greatness. I only hope I can leave the legacy they have.

Last but definitely not least, Cash. My beautiful German Shepherd who sat at my feet the many hours I spent working on this project. Looking up at me with eyes that said I could do anything.

I cannot thank you all enough. Thank You, THANK YOU!

Contents

Patricia Knight

Foreword

By Debrena Jackson Gandy

National Best-selling Author, Speaker, Mentor and Success Coach

In this day and age of too much information bombarding us in too many ways, non-stop and incessantly, it can create overwhelm and have us feel like we're suffocating under perpetual busy-ness and doing-ness. Unfortunately, we can get caught up, like hamsters furiously running on a hamster wheel -- spinning our wheels in our lives, but getting no-where. When we're caught up on the hamster wheel, we're expending a lot of energy, the wheel is turning, we're seeming to make progress, when really, we're going around in circles. Truth be told, this is the case for far too many of us.

More technology, quicker, faster and constantly offering more or upgraded devices, has not delivered on its promise of making life easier or simpler, and certainly not more reward-ing. Actually our lives can feel like they have gotten more complicated, and more over-stimulated and distracted instead – filled with too many things, too much stuff and clutter, too much activity, all which max out the bandwidth in our minds and lives.

This is why the timing on *Move! You're in Your Own Way* is so perfect. We need a way off of the hamster wheel, back to what matters most, and most importantly, we need to find our way back (or for the first time) to what brings us joy, fills

our souls and makes our heart sing. The book is your guide –
it is the light that leads you back to yourself, without being
too high-brow, "coachy," or scientific.

Patricia Knight, as a life coach, has turned over every stone
and included here everything you need to free yourself from
the hamster wheel, and actually start making real and
rewarding progress. Whether it's her sections on being
authentic and knowing yourself, uncovering your passions,
gifts and true values, or clarifying your vision and intentions,
she makes it plain and provides a breath of fresh air with the
simplicity of the exercises and reflections she provides, and
then the sprinkling of personal and client stories that
illuminate key concepts.

She also helps you lovingly look at damaging habits, and
where they are arising from, and supports you in turning to
face, what, in the past, have been your walls, barriers and
roadblocks. And of course, the final ingredient of creating do-
able action steps to the fulfillment of your heart's desires
rounds out this book. She brings together a combination of
compassion and gentleness, and where needed, a firm commitment to having no excuses and holding you accountable.

If you've been looking for a personal coaching guide that
meets you where you are, and takes you to where you want to
go – this is it. Look no further.

Foundation

Why You, Why Me?

Your Path to Extraordinary

I SURVIVED MY EARLY YEARS. There were times when that might have been in question. Many that I grew up with did not. I was blessed to have learned how to overcome many barriers. I am grateful to have gained knowledge and tools creating a path in a different direction.

As a Certified Life Coach for over nine years, I have worked with clients who accomplished much more than they imagined they could. Many of my clients asked me if the principles, tools and information I use to help them were written down anywhere. Now they are.

These strategies were learned from others, my life's learning, my innate skills and talents, my training and education, (I graduated with a degree in Psychology and Math in the top 5% of my class), and from over thirty years of extensive experience in consulting, counseling and case management, project management, training, motivational speaking, program development and long range strategic planning.

By sharing what I have discovered in my life, and the many obstacles I've encountered, I want to offer guidance that may help you discover yourself and achieve whatever you choose to do.

So, what would you really like to achieve?

To live a more balanced life?

Freedom to express your creativity?

Better goal achievement?

Success? Happiness?

More focus?

Overcome barriers

Our desires are different for each of us, but we all travel similar paths. We all have fears, barriers, and limitations. We have questions whose answers are not evident. Or, directions that are unclear. We have to figure out where we want to go and how best to get there.

I assume that you are motivated to live your best life, to achieve your dreams. Yet, a thousand road blocks may stand between you and your dreams. I also believe that you have the capability to create the path you desire and get to where you want to go. This book will help you build a foundation for learning more about who you are and your place in the world. You'll discover how much power you actually have to choose and direct your destiny. You will develop a clear vision and set Intentions that will guide you toward your goals.

Together we will explore the way you think. Your thoughts are the pathway to getting where you want. Command your thoughts and you can overcome barriers and limitations. You will find that a new perception allows you to better control how you take action. Kaleidoscope Life Coaching is named such to exemplify the fact the one small twist, (change of perception) gives a whole new picture. With the knowledge and tools I've discovered, you too can live the fullest life possible. And, you will experience the joy that comes from finally choosing to take care of yourself.

How I Got to Here from There

My life path has been eclectic. Currently, I am a life coach, author, motivational speaker and trainer. My passion is working as a professional life coach. My life is by no means perfect (human perfection is a work of fiction), but it is a very good life. What I have learned and experienced will, I trust, give you fresh ideas and a different perspective.

Like so many, my upbringing was "humble" with few advantages. I was the child of a poor, single mother. I never met or had any interaction with my father; wouldn't know him if I saw him. Although this is an old story repeated many times over with many others, it still took its toll on me. I spent most of my life growing up in the projects. Not the greatest environment, and not many positive examples to emulate. Like many poor families, our level of dysfunction ran deep. My mother worked too hard to have any energy left to provide love, support, encouragement, or the attention I yearned for. In fact, for most of my life I was convinced she didn't even like me. Most of the messages I received from my family and others were, "You can't do anything; you won't amount to anything." Because she worked so much, she left much of my rearing to my brother. He was only two years older and, to put it mildly, was a harsh taskmaster. He was both my protector from the world and a source of extreme punishment. (Talk about confusing messages.)

My brother was just a kid himself and had the same lacks and challenges I did. He could not have exhibited parenting skills he had never seen. (Nor could my mother for that matter.) The harshness I experienced from both mother and brother beat at my spirit. It was part of the continuing message that I had little value. Never in my life was I told I was loved, smart, a good girl, beautiful, destined for something special. Not a good start on building self-esteem. The only time I was told anything was when I did something wrong. Talk about negative messages. One thing I remember is saying to myself defiantly, "You are wrong. I am not what you say I am. I am good, I can do things." (I was a determined little cuss.)

I was saved by the gift of loving books. They were my escape and my teachers. I learned that people were encouraged, they were told they could do the things they wanted. I read about hope, about working toward your desires and about encouragement. I read about people that I wanted to be like. I read about and believed in possibilities. *Although I did not realize it then, I was given my first glimpse of the power of thought and belief. I was not able to use it yet but the seed had been planted.*

My uncertainty about who I was kept me exceptionally shy. I lived in my head and made up my own worlds. I loved being in the library, reading, learning life lessons, dreaming and imagining my world the way I wanted it to be. I was a dreamer, letting my imagination run wild. *I was gifted with my first experience of the power of visualizing.* I spent every possible moment in the library. It was my escape and my sanctuary. I read science fiction, mysteries, encyclopedias, Greek mythology and *Pippi Longstocking*. (*I was* still a kid). I filled my head with even more visions to fuel my imagination. In science fiction I loved possibilities to come. Mysteries helped develop an interest in figuring things out. Other books opened up my view of the world. I was drawn to all kinds of information and learning about anything I didn't know. In the library I read… I dreamed… and I imagined all the ways my life might be. *Little did I know that was the first step toward making my vision real.* One of my first childhood dreams was to become a librarian when I grew up. I thought the most wonderful job possible would be to get paid to read. (Yeah Right.) Then I wanted to be part of a scientific think tank learning about different disciplines of scientific thought and bringing those perspectives to solve problems. (Both incorporated my love of learning, reading, and problem solving. Plus I loved science.) It was not quite a conscious decision, but that's how I first learned I could create my life the way I wanted it to be. I knew I could do it. I saw it as real. I believed it. Not all dreams come true in the way we first believed, but they do teach you about yourself. I never stopped dreaming and believing. And I grew up to have new dreams.

When I was a scant eighteen just out of high school, I became a too-young single mother of a baby girl, a beautiful gift who stole my heart at first cry. I had no money and less help. Still, my view of the world changed in that instant; my vision changed. I was determined to be the best mother I could be, and to show her how much she was cherished and loved. (I did pretty well as she continues to be my joy, and as an adult is my best friend. She is someone I respect and am immensely proud of.) Because of her and for her, I wanted to do more and to give her more. I knew I could not do it on my then low-paying, dead-end job. I believed that I needed something more, an education. At age 24, I quit my job and enrolled at the University of Washington in Seattle. At that time, I was raising my then four year old alone, and working at a barely-over-minimum-wage-paying job. I think I went forward on pure belief. Again, I was given a gift; the ability to see myself where I wanted to go. My love of science and information also served me well. I earned my degree. This barely "C" average high school student graduated with honors at the top of my class. Who knew?

Although never perfect, life has been good. I married then had a devastating divorce. Some years I was in a place so dark, it was hard to breath. Crash and burn would have been an improvement. But somehow I held on to my belief that I could accomplish the things I set out to do. Eventually I did. I achieved success and honors for the work I did (in counseling, marketing, program development and implementation, management, and strategic planning) before training to become a Life Coach.

I was not a librarian, but I have held jobs that I loved. Jobs that needed the skills and abilities that I identified myself with. It is so powerful to fill the job that you believe is made for you. A number of jobs were the stuff of (my) dreams. At one job, I got to ask people in companies, "What do you do?" How do you do it?" (Did I tell you I was curious? Something I got in trouble for as a kid served me well.) To better understand the nature of the company, I needed to learn how they worked and what they wanted to accomplish. Then I helped them improve. I went on tours that were like going on "field trips." (Remember the 5th grade field trip? Major Fun!) At another job I traveled around the country managing a million dollar contract, discovering how enviromnental organizations worked, and figuring out how to help them do it better with my program. I loved figuring things out and making them better. I also discovered I loved to travel. (Adventure is one of my values.) At that job, in my first year, I achieved my yearly goal in only six months and continued to break records. I love mentoring kids and I worked with over 400 youth as a manager of a City program with ten staff. I received a Mayor's Award for outstanding service. My next job allowed me to dream up new projects, then plan and make them happen. One of the projects I created won a national Savvy award.

Much of what I accomplished was by identifying who I was. When younger, I did not know, did not have a clue of my value or my worth. I didn't even know that I could do things well. My first experience of doing honors work in college was an eye opener. I started looking at "what else can I do." I began to learn what my strengths were, what my values are, and how to be Intentional about my next steps (before I truly understood Intentions). Please do not think it was all lightness and joy. Some of these years were the "dark years." The most powerful thing I did even when I had been kicked in the teeth by life was to keep from wavering in my belief that "if it can be done, then I can do it!" Also that things WILL work out.

Here's what helped me. The many times when life around me was challenging, I believed in possibilities and that belief carried me when I could not carry myself. I always saw the vision. I (finally) knew who I was. Also I was gifted with abilities and strengths that I believed were not just for my benefit. I believe all people have a responsibility to share their gifts of knowledge with others.

I gained maturity and had multiple wonderful jobs and experiences that I was grateful to have had .Yet I knew there was more; I desired to do what I was truly meant to do. It was time for a new level. I began the search for what it could be. I set an Intention that I would do what I was destined to do and to be. It took a while and finally I discovered "what I wanted to do when I grew up." I knew a lot about me, I knew the things I really loved to do and then I discovered something I could do that allowed me to do *all* of them: helping people, adults and kids, creating and managing projects, discovering new things, motivating, learning, teaching, and training. Now, I do them all in what is to me a profound and important way. It might be said I found my purpose as a Personal Life Coach and Speaker. I help people who want to reach their full potential and who want to live their best life, to live *their* vision.

This really excites me. Here is my current plan and on-going vision:

> Continue helping people discover how to live at peak performance with my coaching.

> Seeing my books help greater numbers.

Doing leadership development nationally.

Seeing my workshops held nationally (internationally).

Being honored nationally for my work as an expert in the field.

Doing speaking engagements around the country.

Helping youth turn on the light to see their empowered selves.

Specific manifestations of my Intention may morph but I am heading toward it. Goes to show what can happen when you desire to live the life of your vision. Proceed on to the journey to your extraordinary life.

1

Who are You Really? Everything Begins with You

The Authentic You

Knowledge is power. Knowing yourself is the fuel that can allow you greater access to your potential and greater confidence regarding your place in the world.

It is not in the stars to hold our destiny but in ourselves. William Shakespeare

Life's challenges are not supposed to paralyze you, they're supposed to help you discover who you are. Bernice Johnson Reagon

It's not who we are that holds us back, it's who we think we're not. Michael Nolan

Know Thyself

Socrates said "Know Thyself." To be our best and do our best, we need to understand our foundation. That foundation resides in you. Actually, it is you. So, who are you really? In this chapter, let's begin to look deeply into the mirror of yourself. Answer these questions.

• What do you value?

- What are your beliefs?

- What are your life principles?

- What are you passionate about?

- What are your strengths?

- What do you want to improve?

- (What do you wish you could totally throw out the window?)

First, know that you are one in a billion. No one else on the planet is like you—there never has been nor ever will be again. You are magnificence, you are extraordinary. (Do you ever wonder what it would be like if we all lived that truth?) Think of all the good things that you (and the world) are missing if you are not your best you. Whether you live it or not, the truth is **you are already the perfect you.**

Look at yourself like the pieces in a kaleidoscope. When you look in, the image can be pleasing or just OK. Turn the kaleidoscope just a little and you discover a whole new image, a whole new perspective that you marvel at. The pieces inside are the same. They did not change, just the perspective changed.

We are like that sometimes. The picture we see of ourselves is not what we want, or there is something more we want, or we just want a slight change. We don't need to get all new pieces, just get a new perspective.

Like the pieces in the kaleidoscope, we have inside everything we need, and we have everything we need to be happy now. Each of us is whole, capable, resourceful, able, creative, intact. You may have thought otherwise or been told you are not OK. But the truth is: you are not broken or in need of fixing. Maybe all you need is a change in perspective. Many times, we turn the kaleidoscope because we want something more. But it is always about being who we are. You were not created to be ordinary; but it is a choice to be extraordinary.

Discovering Extraordinary

To become extraordinary, let's look at your magnificence in five easy exercises.

> **This is not an exam.** You can write as much or as little as you wish. You might start with a few and come back to the exercises later. You could write one or two. You can write only one. You could just consider the answers in your mind. It's your choice. But it's important that you have knowledge of what your responses may be.

Most of the clients I've worked with find these exercises easy. If you find the exercises difficult, it may even be more important that you complete them. The aim is that each of us should be able to clearly identify and be able to state who we are. To be most effective in life, it's important to know your abilities, what you have a difficult time doing, and your values. This is the first foundational block: knowledge that will give you greater connection and access to your personal power. You are then able to operate from a position of strength, with more confidence, greater self-respect, and peace of mind.

Roles: Exercise One

Write as many self-descriptors (roles you play) as you identify with (most people can do about 25).

For example, my list includes: I am daughter, mother, sister, and friend. I am giving, loving, a fun seeker, curious, adventurous, joy-filled, imaginative, an avid reader, lifelong learner, contributor, hiker, artist, guitar student, author, speaker. Your turn.

"I AM":

_____

_____

_____

_____

_____

_____

_____

_____

_____

_____

_____

Gifts: Exercise Two

List your gifts, the things you *naturally do well.* Some gifts may repeat items from the roles section, that's OK. (Me, I am terminally curious, persistent, a natural problem solver, creative. I have a thirst for knowledge, learn easily, I make friends easily, etc.)

_____

_____

_____

_____

_____

_____

_____

_____

_____

_____

_____

_____

OK, I hope this doesn't feel like a lot of work, but this is all about you. Just a few more exercises. Have fun.

Passions: Exercise Three

List the things you love to do, or did in the past that you enjoyed (personal or professional). These could be two things, five, or even ten. (Mine include: going to aquariums, museums, being in nature, walking at the ocean, having adventures, laughing, helping, motivating and encouraging people, learning, lunching with friends, shopping, etc.)

"I LOVE":

_____

_____

_____

_____

_____

_____

_____

_____

_____

_____

_____

Attributes: Exercise Four

Look at your passion list and determine what attributes are associated with each item. This is a step toward identifying and knowing your passion. For example:

Do you like climbing? Attribute: Adventure/challenge shows up.

Is art important to you? Then creativity and beauty is important to you.

Is exercise a strong love? Then fitness, strength or discipline is your thing.

Is hanging out with friends a priority? You are highly social.

Do you organize your closets and desk just for fun? Organization and order are important.

Do you love problem solving, family, love, or faith? Then....

_____

_____

_____

_____

_____

Abilities: Exercise Five

To ensure you have a well-rounded picture of yourself. List your abilities and strengths gained from your experiences, things you learned to do well or discovered you could do well. (Example, I am a competent project manager, strategist, speaker, planner and writer). You can also take out an old résumé and refer to the experiences listed.

Caution, while it's easy for most of us to identify negative traits or perceived imperfections, this is not the time. Instead, list the attributes the angels sing about, things we think about ourselves but don't think we should pat ourselves on our own shoulders. So go ahead, list those things you are proud of, the things about you that you believe are magnificent.

_____

_____

_____

_____

_____

_____

_____

_____

_____

Broaden the Picture

Muster your courage and ask yourself: How do people see me? I was curious and wanted to get a clear picture not only of who I thought I was, but how the world perceived me. So, after I did these exercises, I asked some close friends to answer these two questions about me:

1. What words would you use to describe me? And

2. What do you think is my greatest attribute?

Their input was interesting. Most of them said the same things that I would have said. But some gave me feedback I had not fully honed in on. Their reactions were awesome and helpful. You might want to do this later.

Identify Your True Values

The individual increasingly comes to know who he is through the stand he takes when he expresses his ideas, values, beliefs, and convictions, and through the declaration and ownership of his feelings. Clark Moustakas

It's not hard to make decisions when you know what your values are. Roy Disney

Another way to stand on the strength of who you are is to know and be firmly grounded in your values. Why? It brings to mind the old saying, if you do not stand for anything, you will fall for everything. Values are the ideals we take strength from and stand upon. Values, beliefs, life principles are what you hold to be true, how you measure your actions and how you interact with the world around you.

Definitions:

Values

Value is a concept that describes the beliefs of an individual.

Values are how we have learned to think things ought to be or people ought to behave.

Values are deeply held beliefs about what is good, right, and appropriate. Values are deep-seated and remain constant over time. We accumulate our values from childhood based on teachings and observations of our parents, teachers, religious leaders, and other influential and powerful people.

Values are traits or qualities that you consider worthwhile; they represent your highest priorities and deeply held driving forces.

Beliefs

Beliefs are the mental acceptance of and conviction in the truth, actuality, or validity of something.

The clearer you are about what you value and believe in, the **happier** and more effective you will be.

Life Principles

Life principles are convictions about life—an accepted or professed rule of action or conduct, a guiding sense of the requirements and obligations of right conduct.

VALUES CLARIFICATION EXERCISE

Effective people identify clear, concise, and meaningful sets of values, beliefs, and priorities. This exercise will help you clarify yours. Read through the following list of qualities and circle **any** that feel particularly important to you. **NOTE, IT DOESN'T MATTER IF THESE ARE NOT ALL STRICTLY "VALUES"**

Abundance	Bravery	Delight	Expertise
Acceptance	Calm	Dependable	Faith
Accomplishment	Candor	Devotion	Family
Achievement	Choice	Direct	Feeling
Action	Clarity	Discernment	Flexibility
Adventure	Comfort	Discovery	Focus
Aesthetics	Commitment	Divinity	Forgiveness
Alignment	Community	Drama	Freedom
Altruism	Compassion	Dream	Fun
Artistic	Competition	Educate	Glamour
Assistance	Completion	Elegance	Grace
Attainment	Conformity	Empowerment	Gratitude
Augment	Congruence	Encouragement	Growth
Authenticity	Connection	Energy	Guidance
Autonomy	Contemplation	Enjoyment	Harmony
Awareness	Contentment	Enlightenment	Health
Awe	Contribution	Entertainment	Holistic
Balance	Control	Excellence	Honesty
Beauty	Courage	Exhilaration	Honor
Bliss	Creativity	Expansion	Hope

Continued on next page.

Humor	Openness	Religious	Touch
Image	Orderliness	Resilience	Transformation
Imagination	Originality	Responsibility	Trust
Improvement	Partnership	Reverence	Truth
Independence	Patience	Risk	Understanding
Influence	Peacefulness	Romance	Uniqueness
Information	Perception	Safety	Unity
Ingenuity	Perfection	Satisfaction	Vision
Inquisitive	Performance	Security	Vitality
Inspiration	Perseverance	Self-expression	Vulnerability
Integration	Personal-	Sensation	Wealth
Integrity	Growth	Sensuality	Wholeness
Intimacy	Persuasion	Serenity	Will
Intuition	Planning	Service	
Invention	Playfulness	Sincerity	
Judgment	Pleasure	Solitude	
Justice	Power	Space	
Laughter	Preparation	Spirit	
Leadership	Privacy	Spirituality	
Learning	Process	Spontaneity	
Love	Professionalism	Stimulation	
Loyalty	Prosperity	Strength	
Magic	Quest	Superiority	
Magnificence	Question	Synthesis-	
Mastery	Radiance	taking	
Movement	Realization	Tenderness	
Mysticism	Recognition	Thinking	
Nature	Refinement	Thoughtfulness	
Nurture	Relationship	Thrill	

List provided by Invite Change training program.

25

Of all the values/qualities that you've circled, write your **TOP TEN** in the space below.

(1)

(2)

(3)

(4)

(5)

(6)

(7)

(8)

(9)

(10)

Now, reduce your list to your **TOP THREE.**

(1)

(2)

(3)

Congratulations! You have identified your critical values upon which all your beliefs stand. Keep them in the forefront of you mind. Values impact every aspect of your life. Additionally, you demonstrate your values in your personal and work behaviors, in decision making, and in social interaction.

You use your values to make decisions about priorities in all areas of your life.

Your goals and life purpose are grounded in your values.

You can use your value list to test new ideas and plans. Do they line up?

The power of knowing values is shown in this story about a client. She had been out of work for months and was frustrated not only from lack of funds but because she no longer wanted to accept a job that had no meaning for her. However, she was not sure where she wanted to go or what she wanted to do. The value exercise served as a filter and helped her eliminate things that did not line up with who she was. Acknowledging and shining the light on her strengths, abilities, and passions reminded her of how good she was. (It also helped boost her lagging confidence due to past failures.) She was open to the possibilities of what she could do and be that lined up with her true values. She went on to find her dream job, using her gifts and lining up with her values.

By doing these exercises, you have begun to uncover new aspects of yourself. I hope you look at the lists and say, "Wow. I am amazing." And you would be right. You are a complex being with many components. Make sure you know and appreciate what all the pieces are. Remember the kaleidoscope. It is even more beautiful when a light is shining through. Knowing who you are is that light.

Now that you have identified the values that are most important to you, the values you believe in and that define your character, the next step is to live them every day in everything you do. Living your values is a powerful way to be the person you want to be, to help you accomplish your vision, your Intentions and your dreams.

Reflection

You now have a good picture of who you are. You have identified what you value, what your strengths are, your passions, your attributes, your roles, and your gifts. Now acknowledge and stand on the truth that you are unique, one in a billion. Actually it is probably closer to one in a trillion. Take a moment to pat yourself on the back and truly appreciate who you are.

Hold this picture of YOU strongly in your mind as you journey through the upcoming sections of Vision, Intentions, Action, Barriers, 100% Living and Taking Care of You. You have created a foundational base of power. Stand on your values, strengths, etc. to help create your vision and set your Intentions. Use them to supply power to your actions, and give you the strength to overcome limitations. Focus on the "best of you" and live at 100%, knowing that you deserve special care.

Also as you work through the different chapters, this knowledge will provide a strong foundation.

2

Vision: Know Where You're Going

What would you do if you could see your future? Visioning helps reveal your future and can help you get there. Keep the picture of "who you are" as you start to create the vision. Remember your gifts, passions, abilities, strengths, and values. Use your magnificence and the knowledge of who you are to help you create your vision.

Extraordinary people visualize not what is possible or probable, but rather what is impossible. And by visualizing the impossible, they begin to see it as possible. Cherie Carter-Scott

To live is to choose. But to choose well, you must know who you are and what you stand for, where you want to go and why you want to get there. Kofi Annan

When you have to make a choice and don't make it, that is in itself a choice. William James

If you do not create your destiny, you will have your fate inflicted upon you. William Irwin Thompson

*All successful people men and women are big dreamers. They imagine what their future could be, **ideal** in every respect, and then they work every day toward their distant vision, that goal or purpose.* Brian Tracy

Your choice is to lead a life that is either proactive or reactive. Proactive means doing what's best for you and making decisions that serve you, controlling your destiny. Being reactive means not deciding, but letting life choose for you without your input, subject to whims of life or life challenges.

Consider that your choices are based on knowing where you want to go and then deciding a path that gets you there? This chapter will help you clarify where you are going and will help you make your vision real.

Don't try to answer these questions, just reflect on them.

- Where do you want to go in life?

- Where will you end up when you get there?

- Where is there?

- What are your goals?

- What are the things that will describe you and your mark on the world?

- What is your vision for your life?

The Bible says, "Without vision the people perish." Your vision is your road map to where you are going. How easy do you think a trip from California to Florida would be if you had no idea what road to take to get there? (Of course, some of us don't know where we want to go. Oh yes, I've been there.)

What would happen if your only focus was on where you came from, as opposed to where you are going? What happens when you continue to look backward as opposed to looking forward while you are driving? Focusing only on the past makes it difficult to go forward. Try driving by looking only in the rear view mirror (actually don't, it's not quite safe). A word of wisdom says, "You'll miss your future looking at your past." Plus focusing only on the past might cause you to crash and burn.

Develop Your Vision, two exercises

Begin - Start planning your roadmap. OK, I know you are thinking, more homework. Think about having fun with it as opposed to feeling the weight of it. Write a letter dated one year from now *about the person you have become in the past year.* List today's month and day, but date it one year from now. Take your time with this. Think about: Where do you live? Who is around you? What do you do when you get up in the morning? What do you see when you look out of your window? What kind of car do you drive? What do your clothes look like? What do you feel good about? Then start writing. You could, for example, start with:

This has been and exciting year. I have_____

_____

Or... Over this last year much has happened. I have been fortunate as I have_____

_____

_____

_____

_____

As you begin the journey of defining your vision, think about these questions:

What would it be like if I could live my vision?

What would it look like?

What would it feel like?

Broaden the Vision

Visualize yourself five years from now, ten, or even twenty years from now. You are at the head table of a family and very close friends, or before a huge crowd where you are standing on a podium getting applause and accolades. Or maybe you are writing your autobiography. *You are the person you wanted to be.* You have left your mark, your legacy. You've accomplished what you set out to do. You have lived your vision.

What are you doing? What are you most proud of? How did you get to the place you are? What is your story? What was the path you took to get to where you are? What did you do? How did you do what you did? What did you think and feel about yourself as you were doing it, (who were you as a person)? Who are you now?

Include all the things you did successfully. (Even think about the things that were a total disaster but you learned from and used the lesson.) What were those lessons? What were some of the things people said about you? Consider the experiences you gained and the skills you developed. Factor in the values you held to be true. Where and how did you use your natural ' gifts and strengths?

Make your visioning as detailed as possible.

Now write the vision. Elaborate, make it real. Details, Details.

_____

_____

_____

_____

_____

_____

_____

_____

_____

_____

Reflection

You now have a clear and distinct picture of who you are as a person. Added is a meaningful, vivid picture of where you want to go and what you will accomplish. Your vision may change over time but know that the very fact that you desire the vision will propel you to it. The next chapter will provide a powerful tool to help you get there.

3

Intentions: Know How You'll Get There

You know who you are. You clarified your vision, painting the picture of what you want in your life. And so, now what? How do you make the vision real? How do you get from where you are to where you want to be, living your vision?

All that counts in life is intention. Andrea Bocelli

Choose your intention carefully and then practice holding your consciousness to it, so it becomes the guiding light in your life. John Roger

Our intention creates our reality. Wayne Dyer

Every journey begins with the first step of articulating the intention, and then becoming the intention. Bryant McGill

Many of us have a desire (maybe even genetically imprinted) to live our highest life, living our purpose and doing the things we were meant to do. What needs to happen? What changes do you need to make? Where does the change begin? What do you do to make your vision a reality?

You set an Intention. An Intention solidifies your visions and plans. An Intention by definition tends to draw you toward it. As you stand in the power of who you are and use the power of your vision, you set your Intention, creating a bridge between your vision and your future.

Think of the negative power that surrounds you when you are faced with an option that does not line up with who you see yourself to be. Then compare that to a situation where you are totally in line with what you believe, in line with your values. Operating in your values empowers you. You will use this power to make your Intention real.

Power of Intention

Most of us are adept at resolving to accomplish particular goals, but there is something even more powerful: **Intentions**. Intentions are greater than the habit of making resolutions or even *just* setting goals. Intentions are stated as positive and are broader, like playing a grand game. Intentions steel you to take an action. With them you set your mind to accomplish a goal and you achieve it.

In the past, I did much goal setting. Never really considering what it meant to me. A goal suggests something attained only by prolonged effort and hardship. Consider the statement, "She worked years to reach her *goals,*" which sounds long and arduous.

So, I submit to you another option. Make an Intention and the Intention will "draw" you toward it.

So, what is it?

> Intention is knowledge of a thing as it is in itself. It is knowledge of the thing as known, a concept considered as the product of attention directed to an object of

knowledge. In the knowing, the mind is said to "intend" or "tend toward" its object.

You can do either: set a goal or an Intention. I invite you to do what will make the greatest difference. You may ask "What is the difference?" And "Why do I care what the difference is?" Take a look. Picture this. It is early morning of the first day of the New Year. You are sitting in a quiet place, with pen and paper in hand, or sitting in front of your computer. You are thinking about your life and the things you think you should do or the things you want to accomplish to be more successful. You think of the New Year's resolutions you'll make and resolve to accomplish particular goals.

Consider your last New Year's resolutions. Think about one or two you have made in the past. How many resolutions did you drop or forget about before spring? (How many did you drop the third week of the year?) As you consider making another resolution, you know that you don't want to do the same old thing. Not another empty resolution. Consider the following:

1. Resolutions do not work when they are something *you think you should* do or even something you *think you should stop doing.*

2. They do not work when they are something *that others* define as success: what your job expects, what your family or friends expect, things that come from outside ourselves.

3. Also, they are limiting: specific, measurable and dated. If you don't do it the way you said, you fail. When you do not do what you said, you fail. When you do not do it when you said you would, you fail. You either are successful or you're not. You succeed or you fail.

4. Also they do not work when they do not line up with your true values and honor the things that are truly important. (You can resolve to be a better person by helping feed the homeless, but your true passion is helping youth be their best. Doing the first may help you feel good, but doing the second will truly serve you.)

Align Intention and Vision

So do something that has more power. Set an Intention.

An Intention is an envisioned, desired future outcome or result.

Again, an Intention is desired and envisioned.

> • Desired. What is the vision you desire? Why do you desire it? What are the values in your life that it honors?

> • Envisioned. Use your vision to make it real. Know how it will work for you. What do you want to do to accomplish it? In what areas of your life would you like greater levels of satisfaction?

Examples

You may be one of many who want to lose weight. Some wish to get more exercise. Others wish to be more focused toward achieving a desire. Look at this process example of a common Intention.

The first step, ask (and answer) Why LOSE WEIGHT?

You reply you desire to be healthier.

So (although it seems obvious) next ask, why be healthy?

So that I can do fun activities: play outside with my kids, see my grandchildren grow up.

Or, I want to live to a healthy active old age, because I love the outdoors and want to hike and camp.

Or another weight loss desire might be to look good. Why?

I want to gain greater confidence.

Again, why?

Because I am more able to do the work I do as a public figure.

With increased confidence, I step out and show up stronger.

Why?

Because I am better able to provide for the family that I love.

Because I am better able do the things I love to do.

I really want to be healthy and be a blessing to my family. I want to feel like the person I believe myself to be.

For each example, the last responses are strong Intentions for one's life.

Start developing your Intention by thinking about your vision, (go back to what you developed in the previous chapter). Ask yourself why you want to accomplish that vision, not just the obvious or surface reasons. You will want to "drill" down to what is the real truth. One real truth in the desire to lose weight was to provide for family.

Here's an example of this process I experienced while coaching a woman who was unhappy with her husband.

My client was upset when her husband did not pick up their daughter as promised. She was extremely angry and she wanted to "have it out" with him. My task was to guide her down a path to set an Intention that would serve her and the situation.

1. My first question to her was "What do you want to say to him so he will know what you feel and what you need?" She said she wanted to tell him how upset she was that he did not pick up their daughter.

2. I then asked "What about that was the most disappointing to you." She said she was mad because he did not do what he promised.

3. I asked, "What about him not doing as he said was so upsetting?" (She was getting more and more tense with me as she felt it was obvious.) I asked her again and she said she

wanted him to do what he said he would do.

4. I asked "What about that was most important?" She said that she needed to know he would follow through.

5. I asked why? "So I know I can trust him."

It was at that point she realized it was all about her need to depend on and trust him which was challenged by past issues in their relationship. The real issue! She knew then what she truly desired. She desired to have a loving, non-challenging (non-accusatory) conversation. She desired the conversation to communicate her needs in such a way that she would be heard. She envisioned a conversation that would result in something positive for both of them. Her Intention was to have a conversation resulting in a greater level of trust and intimacy. Operating in that Intention, she was able to have the conversation which she later reported was a wonderful success. Both she and her husband understood each other and reached new levels of closeness.

The reason to "drill down" to the true reason behind the desire is to find what strikes a chord and lines up with your values. Sometimes it is evident in the beginning.

For example, another person I worked with had an Intention to build leadership in diverse communities.

Why?

So others are inspired to do the same.

Why?

So the world is a better place, one community at a time.

Why?

So young girls like I used to be have opportunities.

And there it was.

This was the true reason behind the desire. Because of her background, this is what she truly wanted, what she believed her purpose and life work to be. She had a strong vision that it was her purpose. So her Intention was clear. The underlying reason is what drove her, the true desire was to help young girls like she was, poor and without advantages have a future. Her reason behind the Intention would draw her.

As you develop your Intention ask yourself as many "whys" as necessary to truly feel you have discovered the true motivation. You will then understand and know how to power your Intention. Drill down to the "nitty-gritty" truth, the true underlying reason. Use the *envisioned* reason and your strong *desire* to pull you toward your vision. **Note:** Keep the Intention process in mind. You will find in the next chapter that you can set an Intention for many areas of your life.

Reflection

An Intention draws you to it. Bear in mind, there is power in belief (you will hear more about this in following chapters). Make your Intention real in your mind. Then live as if it were real. I have a wall plaque in my kitchen that I love, which says, "Believe and act as if it were impossible to fail."

With Intentions, you cannot fail. By definition you are always "tending toward the objective." You can change an Intention or you can modify it, or you can go for another one. There is no failure, only forward action. With Intentions, mistakes or missteps are opportunities to begin again, more intelligently. With Intentions you do not demand perfection, instead you relax and pursue the excellence of the journey.

4

Take Action: Make Sure You Get There

Nothing happens until you move. Take action! You are firmly grounded in your authentic you, your values, and your vision. Your foundation is strong. Now you will take actions to empower your steps.

When it is obvious that the vision cannot be reached, don't adjust the vision, adjust the action steps. Confucius

I have been impressed with the urgency of doing. Knowing is not enough; we must apply. Being willing is not enough; we must do. Leonardo da Vinci

A vision is a dream with its feet on the ground. Unknown

A vision without action is just a Dream. Nelson Mandela

Visions and Intentions are building blocks that disappear like mist in the morning unless action is taken. How do you make Intentions work for you? Choose the actions that will support it.

FIRST THING FIRST

Keep your vision and the important Intentions you have in the forefront of your mind. You have already done the exercises that clearly articulate what and why. You have a strong desire and have envisioned the outcome.

Now you will set and evaluate the priorities in your life. The best way to accomplish what you set out to do is to align your Intentions with your whole life in mind. You will look at how your priorities line up with your values. You will consider your gifts, passions and strengths. And you will do it with your whole life in balance.

As you look at the areas of your life that are important to you, you will gauge the areas where you would like greater levels of satisfaction. You will develop and be grounded in the Intention for the area. You will make action choices to support what you want to accomplish that will make the vision real.

The Wheel of Life

The following is a "Wheel of Life," containing sections labeled with various possible life priorities. You may use the ones here or change some of the section labels to better reflect *your* whole life and priorities. You are to pick a section, and think about *your current level of satisfaction in that area.* As you think about the level of satisfaction, consider a scale of zero to one hundred percent. What is your level of satisfaction?

Examples

1. You look at your vocation and know there is more you want to do, different things you want to do, but you are doing pretty well on the job and you feel all right. You think about your family and feel like work has taken so much of your time that you are neglecting them. But you know that if you can do this for a while, you will be able to provide your family with

something that is important to them, such as a new home or promised vacation. You believe it is important and your family supports all of your hard work and effort. Your vocation level of satisfaction is 70%.

2. Another example of plotting the wheel is the person who is considering his family section. He may be working too many hours and feel he has broken promises to do things with or go places with the family. He is coming home late most evenings and the children are already asleep. His spouse is upset and complaining. For this person the family section level of satisfaction is 40%. (Interesting how the situations of working long hours are the same but with different effects.) Both examples are plotted on the following wheel.

Your Life

Change any section label and replace it with another if it fits more with your life. *Look at each topic area on your wheel and assign a percentage.* There is no right or wrong, no judgment. You are looking at only what would give YOU greater satisfaction, where you want more. And it is only how you feel right now, at this moment. It might be different next month or next year.

Mark your choice on the wheel by drawing a line that represents the percentage, with zero being the wheel's core and 100% at the outside edge. Do the exercise for each section on the wheel. Fill in the space under the line as in the examples above.

As you look at your wheel, picture the ride—Smooth—Bumpy—Impossible. Whatever you see, know that you have total control and can make the wheel the way you want it to be. You have the absolute, unmitigated, complete ability to achieve more of what you want in any area of your life. You are whole, capable and resourceful and you have all the tools you need.

Increasing Satisfaction

Now let's get to what you want more of.

Start by picking *only* two or three areas from your wheel that you want to work on now. Choose whatever you want. It may not even be your greatest Intention. It could be the thing that will get you there. Also, you have to start somewhere. No one can tackle the whole world at one time. You are in control. Pick what you really want to work on now. **For now, just fill in the choice line and ignore the lines following the choices. They will be filled in later.**

Choice   **1.**

_____

_____

_____

_____

_____

_____

Choice

2.

_____

_____

_____

_____

_____

_____

Choice

3.

_____

_____

_____

_____

_____

_____

Six Steps to Action

1. Look at your selections and do a quick check. Think about how they line up with your values, your vision and your Intentions. Make whatever notations you choose under each choice.

2. Next, as you choose one you want to start with, visualize what success will look like. Visualize what will give you great-

er levels of satisfaction. Remember making the vision real is always an important step.

Now the work begins. Look at your picks and think about what things *you want to do to* achieve a <u>greater level of satisfaction</u>.

3. Create possibilities by brainstorming and coming up with a list of possible options of things you could do to increase satisfaction, from the wild to the logical and well-defined. Come up with as many as you can.

4. Make a choice. Of those items you brainstormed, what are you willing to do? (Remember to make proactive choices.) These are not the things you think you should do but the things you *want* to do.

5. Take action. Exactly how will you follow through with your selected proactive choice? Forward the action with planning. Do the first thing that takes you quickly to action.

6. Anchor your choice. You have a plan, so now consider what you can do to "anchor" your commitment to action.

Anchoring definition - Steadfastly secured, a rigid point of support. A source of security or stability. To hold fast.

You have possibly stepped outside your comfort zone or at least into new areas. You do not want your choices to fade so you will want to anchor them. Increase the strength of your follow-through.

A tool I use with clients to help them anchor their choices is to make a **"So that... I will...."** statement.

State the action choice, followed by the Intention it supports or why it is important to you, anchoring your choice to your Intention, vision.

Client examples

So that my responses are respectful and well received, building greater credibility at my job **I will** pause and think before responding.

So that I will continue on my path to increased health and well-being, **I will** walk 20 minutes a day.

So that my family knows how important they are, **I will** plan dinner and games with them every Friday.

Keep the statement firmly in mind as a way to anchor yourself to your path.

Think of other ways that will help you commit, anchor and remember your choice. Do you have something that will serve as a reminder? Will you put up a reminder sign? Is there an item you can carry in your pocket as a reminder? Do whatever will work for you.

Whatever we put our attention on will grow stronger in our life. Maharishi Mahesh Yogi

I.A.A.D.

The formula is, **Intention**, plus **Attention**, and **Action**, equals you manifesting your **Desires**. (I+A+A=D)

Make your Intention, determine to put your attention on it, have a plan of action, and achieve your desires.

Single Daily Action, (SDA)

Here is another easy tool to help you toward success. What one small action can you choose to do each day this coming week toward your action plan?

• One client chose health as an area of his wheel where he wanted greater satisfaction. He chose an SDA that would help him live a long life so that he could see his children grow up and have children, as well as be able to help raise them. His parents died young and his children never knew them. His commitment to making a change was to walk at least 20 minutes a day and drink eight ounces of water upon arising.

• Another client whose upbringing was one where she received many negative comments, desired to change the negative messages that diminished her self-esteem. She choose to take one minute while brushing her teeth to tell herself how pleased she was with who she had become and the choices being made in her life.

They both made other choices and built upon them over time, adding success upon success.

Choose one thing you can do (want to do) each day for seven days. Next week, change your SDA to another action that will support you. Or, add another to the existing one. Then another and another. Your choice.

Reflection

One small change at a time can make a major difference over time. Think about an ocean liner whose captain makes a direction change only a few degrees to the right. At first there is negligible difference, but over a period of time the difference is huge and the course has been changed.

You know what strengthens and empowers you. You are able to look at your life and make decisions to work on priorities. You've created an action plan, as well as devised ways to keep moving forward. The next chapter will aid you in identifying and overcoming barriers to success.

5

Walls, Barriers and Roadblocks: Don't Let Them Stop You

Fear! Doubts! Lack of confidence! Guilt! Multiple obstacles can stand between you and where you want to go. This chapter shows how barriers are constructed and how to deconstruct or work around them. How you choose to view obstacles will make it easier or harder to go around (under, over, or through) them. Meeting and overcoming your roadblocks serves to both challenge and strengthen you.

If you're trying to achieve, there will be roadblocks. I've had them; everybody has had them. But obstacles don't have to stop you. If you run into a wall, don't turn around and give up. Figure out how to climb it, go through it, or work around it. Michael Jordan

Success is to be measured not so much by the position that one has reached in life as by the obstacles which he has overcome. Booker T. Washington

Stand up to your obstacles and do something about them. You will find that they haven't half the strength you think they have. Norman Vincent Peale

There are plenty of difficult obstacles in your path. Don't allow yourself to become one of them. Ralph Marston

Obstacles are like wild animals. They are cowards but they will bluff you if they can. If they see you are afraid of them... they are liable to spring upon you; but if you look them squarely in the eye, they will slink out of sight. Orison Swett Marden

You have had an opportunity to use the tools in the prior chapters to become adept at:

Knowing your authentic you and standing on the foundation of your abilities.

Creating the vision to know where you are going.

Setting the Intention and understanding the why of your desire.

Aligning all with your authentic you.

Taking action to give yourself a greater level of satisfaction while considering your whole life.

You may wonder, "If I know all this, why is everything not perfect?" (If you are fortunate and have things perfect, congratulations. But read the rest anyway for when barriers surface.)

What stands in your way of achieving your vision? Again, except for that most perfect person (who probably does not exist), all of us have experienced obstacles or barriers. Some come from outside of us, some from our current environment, some from within. Knowing and identifying the barriers and self-imposed limitations are the first steps to overcoming them.

1st Barrier: Pre-programming
How it Begins

Consider what's on your mind right this minute. What's in there? Well, during the day, we think about too many things to even remember. And, what you recall are the things you are *aware* of thinking about. Things also exist that we don't think about. These are the pre-programmed thoughts of the subconscious mind, our tapes. Each of us has recorded messages in our minds, similar to tape recordings. Yes, we all have them. Consider how these come about, why, and what our minds *still* believe.

All of us have a certain amount of programming that began in childhood and started to define who we were going to become. The subconscious programming in your mind comes from multiple sources, your parents, siblings, teachers, other children, friends, or your mate. Even strangers on the street can influence the way we think of ourselves. The teacher who said, "I know this is hard for you but you just don't work hard enough." Or the one who said, "You should be in another class because you cannot do this one." Or the stranger who looked sideways at you as you entered the upscale establishment as if you did not belong.

Maybe it was a kid in grade school who laughed when you made mistakes and called you dumb. Or a friend who invited everyone else to his party but you (some friend). It was the many slights, the negative feedback, even the lack of positive feedback. It might have been yourself who looked in the mirror and decided you did not look as good as the next person. It may have even been a parent who said, "Stop that, you will only get hurt" when you were being adventurous.

Some information was told to protect us, some was true at a moment in time, some was due to particular circumstances, and some not true at all. Some of the most persistent, insideous messages, we have told to ourselves. We can't even blame it on someone else. (Have you ever looked in the mirror and told yourself you look ugly or too fat?)

The programming does not know that we have grown beyond some things. It does not know the difference between the right or wrong, or the things that may have been true but are not any longer. It just knows what it knows and, like a tape, it replays the message it has received.

Remember when you were told not climb the monkey bars: "You'll be hurt." You learned that there was danger in the world and there are things you should not do. Then there is:

You can't do that!

That's too hard for you!

You'll never learn anything that hard!

Don't try that, you will fail!

You'll be disappointed! Or worse...

That's horrible!

You can't do anything!

Why do you think you can do that?

That's dumb! Or even worse yet...

You're dumb!

You're too fat/too thin!

You're not pretty/handsome enough!

You're not good enough!

You don't really belong here!

You'll never be able to...

You can't do this, you can't do that, YOU CAN'T!!!

Some of the messages made us fearful, many of the messages told us we were less than perfect, that others were better, and caused us to doubt ourselves and our abilities. Some of the message came veiled. Some came loud and clear.

The secret doubts make us think that to truly be who we want to be, we must do something, get more education, lose weight, gain weight, get a better job, work less, work more, be more successful, or achieve a particular goal in our future. In other words, do something different or be something different. These messages undermine our confidence when we are on a mission.

I think of the Pig Pen cartoon character in Charles Shultz's Charlie Brown comic. Pig Pen was the dirty-faced little kid who walked around with a cloud of dirt around him. Wherever he walked, the dust surrounded him. When he moved, the dust moved, it was ever a part of him. All of our negative thoughts are like little specks of dust. All of the couldn'ts, shouldn'ts, and wouldn'ts, create specks of dust.

Too hard, a speck of dust.

Too dumb, another speck of dust.

Too much fear and doubt, another speck.

Too....

These specks form an invisible cloud that follows and influences you, enough that you have a cloud much like Pig Pen character. That cloud surrounds and prevents you from being your best. The cloud is self-doubt, negative feedback, and past failures. That cloud, however invisible, exerts its power.

How it Manifests

As negative programming grows, or just continues over time, the "cloud" forms itself into "The Gremlin." The Gremlin comes with a nagging, negative voice from a place deep inside your subconscious, the voice that embodies all of the negative programming, the doubt and fears, the voice that whispers to you at the most unlikely times. Times when you are considering learning something new or setting a new goal. It whispers to you when you start in a new challenging direction that requires risk, vulnerability, or courage and major planning. You work through the steps of your plan, then in a pause, the voice of the Gremlin surfaces. (Remember back in June, last year, when you tried to do something like this and you failed?) Sometimes it doesn't even speak, it reruns the old tapes. The Gremlin voice is an echo of the past; its doubting entity may have absolutely no basis in truth now. What form does Gremlin take? It could be a huge Goliath, a tiny devil on your shoulder whispering in your ear, a monster in the closet, a wise guy with a smart mouth, a Prim and Prissy miss who can only do what is "proper," or maybe a rolling ball of uncertainty. Maybe you see it as another part of you that has a different voice. The other side of you that says "I don't wanna do that." It may manifest its voice with an "I want what I want" personality. The most insidious is the voice we don't even hear, the tape that just makes us doubt.

At times we let the voice of our Gremlin, the negative voice undermining our desires, goals, or confidence, scream loudly in our ears. It says (while jumping up and down on your shoulder or on your ego), other people who started where you started are farther ahead of you. Other people are doing it better than you. You should have already done this.

No matter how your Gremlin manifests itself, consider the fact that it is like Goliath, and Goliath was just a bully. What Goliath do you have in your life who stops you from accomplishing the things that are important to you? A bully can impact you only if you give it the power to do so.

You can learn tools to better understand your Gremlin, to communicate with it and to reverse its messages to you. Whatever form your Gremlin takes, learn to recognize it when it makes itself known. Like David and Goliath, you can then bring it down, breaking its influence.

Breaking down Barrier 1

Whatever you hold in your mind will tend to occur in your life. If you continue to believe as you have always believed, you will continue to act as you have always acted. If you continue to act as you have always acted, you will continue to get what you have always gotten. If you want different results in your life or your work, all you have to do is change your mind.

To vanquish your Gremlin your first step is to make the decision that you will not let it rule your life. Decide you will be victorious and negate its power. Even if you are not sure how you will do it, set the Intention, decide that it will happen. (Remember the programming is a tape that just wants to replay itself; it does not know the difference between right and wrong, true or false. Its only power is to rerun what it knows.)

The next step is to learn how to identify your Gremlin(s).

How does **your** Gremlin manifest itself?

Draw and it or describe it. What is it like, how does it show up?

This Gremlin is a Red Eyed Monster who makes you envious of everyone while saying "They can do _____, but you can't. It also says, you can try and try and just like before, You Will Fail!

Your Gremlin may present itself as a dark, menacing blob or a mean puritanical-looking matron.

As best you can, draw or describe *your* Gremlin...

Take Power over Your Gremlin

Building awareness of your Gremlin is the first step toward clearing its influence. You have begun to learn to identify what your Gremlin is like (domineering, fearful, an automatic naysayer, etc).

Next, as you decided you will not let its voice influence you, take steps to learn how to "communicate" with it. (Remember words have power.) Choose an action that works for you to respond to your Gremlin. Examples:

> You can acknowledge the Gremlin then put it away, saying you hear it but choose to do something different.

> You can kick it to the side or just tell it to "Take a long walk off a short pier."

You may metaphorically stomp it.

You can send it to the end of the universe.

You can imagine it getting smaller and smaller.

You can say, "I hear you but you just do not get a vote."

Or you may say, *"Thank you very much, it's not the case that I'm not as good as I want to be, I'm just not as good as I'm going to be."*

List 3 tactics for dealing with your Gremlin. What messages will you use to communicate with it?

1.

2.

3.

F.L.I.P. It (and Failure Loses Its Power)

This is a tool I use with clients (and myself) all the time. When I hear something presented in the negative or disempowering way my request is to "F.L.I.P. It." This is another way to deal with the Gremlin. You **"FLIP"** the Gremlin message by the use of empowering language. Empowering language is exactly what it says: language that gives you power, gives you the extra edge. It is the opposite of negative self-talk. Consider dark and light. Dark is the negative language, light the empowering. Light and dark cannot exist in the same space. Dark is the absence of light. If there is light, dark cannot exist. Empowering language and negative dis-empowering language cannot exist in the same space.

You can FLIP the message and change the power in your life by changing what you say. Try changing the negative words to positive and see your reality change with the power of your words. Give it a try. List some of your challenges, things you want to do but you felt doubt or fear around. Now change any negative thoughts into empowering positives (FLIP it). Examples

I am always late—I arrive on time or early.

I learn slowly—I have a mind that absorbs knowledge.

I can be so flaky—I am disciplined.

I am unsure of myself—I am confident.

Everything seems so beyond me—I open new doors of possibilities.

I don't always know what to do next—I am focused and clear.

I can't lose weight—I am eating to lose weight.

I make a mess every time I try to do that—It is amazing what I can do when I try and work hard.

Negative messages from Your Gremlin "Flip It"

_____   _____

_____   _____

_____   _____

_____   _____

_____   _____

_____   _____

_____   _____

_____   _____

_____   _____

_____   _____

The following are examples of Flipped thoughts and statements about my life. Some are the definition of me, some are easy, and some are part my ongoing journey:

I am successful.

I am intelligent and creative.

I set Intentions, take action and achieve my goals.

I am giving and compassionate.

I let go of anger, fear and resentment.

I am loved and cherished by others.

I am healthy.

I eat nutritious foods.

I exercise my body regularly.

I develop my mind and faith.

I am grateful and optimistic.

I choose to live my best life.

I am ONEderful, unique and divine.

I am the author of an extraordinary life.

It all starts with words: Your Words. What power would you add to your life by believing this is true? When you begin to speak to yourself in a more positive way, stopping negative self-talk, FLIPing to language that supports and empowers you, you have a way to stop messages from the Gremlin and take away its power.

2nd Barrier- Controlling Thoughts

Our preprogramming often sets us up to have *unconscious* negative thoughts. We perpetuate them with our *conscious* thoughts. Unlike preprogramming which creates unconscious tapes, we have more control over our thoughts than we imagine!

Remember when we were kids and thought we could do anything. We could be whatever we wanted to be: president, astronaut, fireman, cowboy, doctor. We thought that we were invincible, that we could achieve any crazy dream we set our minds to. We never entertained the thoughts of failure. Many of us were like that even in our teens, twenties, and beyond.

I was always a dreamer and didn't know then it was the early versions of visions and Intentions. Remember my story? When I was 23, a single mother of a four-year-old daughter, without a penny in the bank, without the encouragement of anyone I knew who had ever done it, I decided to attend the University of Washington and earn a degree. Somehow it never entered my mind that I may not be accepted, that I would have to come up with the money to pay for it, or that I might not be able to get the grades to succeed. I never even thought of the multitude of challenges to overcome. My only thought was: "I can do this." Side note here: it was not always a piece of cake and sometimes it seemed more than I could handle. But I continued to believe it could be done and that I could do it. And I did!

If I had thought about how difficult it was to go to college, how expensive it was, how hard it would be to do it and care for my daughter, the story may have had another ending.

How powerful could we all be if we had the thoughts we had as kids and went for it? Many people actually live their thoughts from childhood. One of my granddaughters, at age 3, said she would be a doctor. She loved anatomy books even then. She now has completed two years of college and already is planning which medical school to attend. The other granddaughter loved and just wanted to play basketball. On a four-year scholarship, she just graduated. Her ongoing plan is play professional women's basketball.

Too many of us lose the belief we had then. I am grateful I always believed the best (well I did have some of what I call my dark ages), but I was blessed to come back to my sense of wonder, that strong belief in possibilities. I was called a "Pollyanna", thought to have a permanent case of rose-colored-glasses, a person terminally optimistic.

You can live your positive beliefs. You must think it, and believe it. You have the ability to create new thoughts, new words, new actions, new behaviors, and new habits.

What are You *Thinking* about Yourself?

Things we have said to ourselves like "I can't," or "I hate the way I look," or "how stupid am I," and similar others are *conscious* negative Gremlin feeders. Conscious expressions! The way you think and what you tell yourself comes into being in your life.

The Bible says, *As a man thinketh, in his heart so is he.*

In *Law of Attraction*, Michael Losier writes: *Universal energy responds to the vibrations* (vibes) you are offering, whatever it is; *Positive attracts positive and negative attracts negative.*

Faith healer Dr. Willard Fuller says, *We walk in the atmosphere of our own believing.*

Different schools of thought agree: You are what you think you are, you have what you say you have, and you can do what you say you can do. A powerful life starts with your thoughts and words.

I cannot say this enough: *many of the limitations you face in life are self-imposed. What you think about yourself can either move you forward or keep you behind a wall, a self-imposed barrier. It's all about your thoughts. You can change your thoughts, and by doing so, change your life.*

We are what we think, said Buddha.

Change your thinking, change your life, said Ernest Holmes.

If you think you can, you can. If you think you can't, you're right, said Mark Twain.

There are many cautions about changing negative thoughts. Yet, we are human. We do not always think in a way that gives us power. Some thoughts are automatic or even deeply embedded. But, there is hope. This barrier we can overcome. Just as the programming tape in our subconscious can be changed with a new message, we can think new thoughts that give us the power to go forward. Think of the difference it would make if you thought of what you *can* do instead of what you *cannot.* Try it. When you catch yourself thinking: This is too hard, I can't do it, it is too hard to learn this. Change the thought to: I have the energy and determination to study and learn until I am proficient. When the thought arises that I have never been able to _____ (whatever it is), change it to *This is a new thing that I will soon be able to do.* (Yup, the F.L.I.P. It exercises at work again.)

I challenge you to change your negative thoughts to positive ones, and attract the positive in your life.

Put in a new tape by focusing on the thoughts you want and the words you say. Think differently and get different results.

The outcome is: you change your Life.

Think of it this way: your words and thoughts are mirrors, what one says, the other believes. You believe it just because you say it. Choose your thoughts. They can be empowering or disempowering.

A variation of this quote has been attributed to the Bible, Buddha, Mahatma Gandhi, Bishop Beckwaith, Ralph Waldo Emerson and the past president of Bi-Lo Stores, Frank Outlaw. I have heard similar versions in lectures and church sermons. Wherever it came from, it is valuable to keep in mind:

Watch your thoughts, for they become words.

Watch your words, for they become actions.

Watch your actions, for they become habits.

Watch your habits, for they become character.

Watch your character, for it becomes your destiny.

More simply put, THOUGHTS->WORDS->ACTIONS-> HABITS ->CHARACTER ->DESTINY. You have the power to change any one of them to impact the others. And in case you have not read enough quotations that focus on your thoughts, here are a few more of my favorites.

They can because they think they can. Virgil

All that we are is the result of what we have thought. The mind is everything. What we think we become. Buddha

Your mind can focus on fear, worry, problems, negativity or despair. Or it can focus on confidence, opportunity, solutions, optimism and success. You decide. Don Ward

It isn't what you have, or who you are, or where you are, or what you are doing that makes you happy or unhappy. It is what you think about. Dale Carnegie

If you realized how powerful your thoughts are, you would never think a negative thought. Peace Pilgrim

What you think about and hold in your mind will tend to occur in your life. If you continue to think as you have always thought, you will continue to act as you have always acted. If you continue to act as you have always acted, you will continue to get what you have always gotten. (Albert Einstein said the definition of insanity is doing the same thing over and over and over and expecting different results!) If you want different results in your life, you have to do something different, change your thoughts.

Breaking Down Barrier 2: Thoughts Can Change

I have described how powerful thoughts can be, now I want to share how to change them so they work for you. But first I will present information supporting the contention that thoughts can be changed.

Over time we have come to believe "It is what it is." Most of us think that the way we think and respond is the only option we have. We believe that our normal response is "sealed in cement" and unchangeable. Different disciplines suggest that thoughts can be changed. Consider the fields of study that support the idea of changing our thoughts.

1. Quantum Physics

2. Law of attraction

3. Brain Plasticity

4. Neuro-linguistic Programming

Some of these ideas are held as incontrovertible, some are controversial. I believe there is more than a grain of truth, if not absolute truth in some of these. I believe the power of thoughts can make major changes and impacts in your life. If you are non-left-brained and not interested in the science (or pseudo-science as you may choose to believe) and happy to just believe, then you might want to skim to the end of the chapter. Otherwise, hang on for some interesting information that is compelling.

SCHOOLS OF THOUGHT

1. Quantum Physics

"Limits exist only in the mind." I contend that what we choose to put our attention on can be impacted. If you set an Intention (Chapter 3), put action behind that Intention (Chapter 4), then you will manifest your desires. Quantum Physics seems to agree.

Quantum Physics, the study of the behavior of matter and energy, suggests that a system changes simply by observing it. This may sound like hocus pocus, but some scientists are coming to believe that just thinking about something can make it happen.

Some background. Quantum physicists found that when firing very small electron particles through two slits, if the electrons were observed while going through the slits, then they acted different then when not observed.

So what could that mean for us?

Your brain sends electrochemical signals. The implications of this are huge. Our act of observation and thoughts affect (the signals and) our world. Our expectations, thoughts and beliefs literally form the world around us.

The fact that our thoughts, emotions, expectations and beliefs can influence, alter, and create reality is what the theory of Quantum Physics may be teaching. Remember "IAAM," Intention plus Attention and Action equals Manifestation. This scientific idea supports that idea. Expand your beliefs and see what can happen when you put your attention on your vision.

It is important to know that I am not saying you are guaranteed to have a specific outcome because you focus on it. As you will see in the chapter on action, you will have to walk your walk. And keep in mind, there will be both good and yucky (technical term) stuff in your life. **But I believe you have a choice in surrounding yourself with energy that is positive and it will bring positive outcomes into your life.**

*When we **think** of failure, failure will be ours. If we remain undecided, nothing will ever change. All we need to do is want to achieve something great and then simply to do it. Never **think** of failure. For what we **think**, will come about.* Maharishi Mahesh Yogi

2. Power of the Law of Attraction

The Law of Attraction (Michael J. Losier, Philip F. Harris, Mike Dooley, Esther Hicks, Wayne Dryer, Jack Canfield and others), says, and it is deceptively simple, *thoughts become things and energy attracts like energy!*

It says, and I believe this to be true, that everything in this universe is "Energy." This energy vibrates at various frequencies. Note: Everything is made up of atoms which have a complex *and* simple structure. The electron itself is energy, and energy is never at rest. Its movement could be called its vibrational power or force. I (and others) would venture to postulate that there are strong vibrations and weak vibrations. Even positive vibrations and negative vibrations.

The nature of the vibrations is to "attract" themselves to vibrations of a similar frequency. In other words, one "cluster" of energy attracts itself to other "clusters" of energy in which it is in vibrational resonance; like is attracted to like. This happens on both a very small and very large scale. For our purposes, we are talking about the idea that our thoughts have a vibrational power to draw what they think about, "that thoughts create our reality."

What do you think happens to the person who sees only the negative in life, and talks about only the negative? I speculate, and have seen many examples, that what they draw toward them is exactly what they expect. When they expect to be treated rudely, ignored by people with a bad attitude, it seems they do not rest until that happens and then they say, "See, I told you that bad thing would happen."

Opposite them are those who look at the world with the belief that it is good. They see there is joy to be had, and things work out for the good. That is exactly what happens for them. Their focus is on the positive things in their life. It is not the case that their lives lack any negative, it is more that they accept and move past the negative with their focus on all that is good in their life.

3. Neuroplasticity

You _can_ re-wire the neural pathways of your brain. Neuroplasticity or brain plasticity refers to the brain's ability to CHANGE throughout life. The brain has the amazing ability to reorganize itself by forming new connections between brain cells (neurons). Amazing work in this area can be seen in books by Norman Doidge, M.D., John B. Arden, Joe Dispenza, Jeffrey Schwartz, M.D. and others.

Research shows that the brain never stops changing through learning. Plasticity IS the capacity of the brain to change with learning. Changes associated with learning occur mostly at the level of connections between neurons. New connections can form and the internal structure of the existing synapses can change. The human brain is able to continually adapt and rewire itself. Even in old age, it can grow new neurons.

Think about going down a slide on a snowy hill. As you go

the same route, you create a groove. The more you go down the hill on the same path, the groove gets deeper. This is much like our thoughts or habits, actions repeated over and over. OK, what happens when halfway down the hill we want to go left, or right? It's difficult to turn the slide and get out of the groove. Note: it is difficult, not impossible. Just as we can work on turning the slide and eventually get out of the groove path, you can change a habit or a thought by the same effort. It takes a bit of work. (Remember the vision, and the Intention? Refer to the chapter on Action to see how to set a new path.)

The following are suggestions to keep your brain active and working. You will want to get in the habit of creating new neural pathways.

Try neural building and strengthening exercises with everyday movements. Use your opposite hand to brush your teeth, dial the phone or operate the TV remote. Change the hand that works your computer mouse.

Keep your brain active with new experiences: travel, expose yourself to different environments, "expand your horizons."

It is extremely important to challenge your brain to learn new and novel tasks, especially processes that you've never done before. Try line-dancing, chess, tai chi, yoga, or painting. Learn to play a musical instrument or learn a new language. You choose.

4. Neuro Linguistic Programming

Neuro Linguistic Programming (NLP for short) was developed in the early 1970s by an information scientist and a linguist at the University of California at Santa Cruz, John Grinder and Richard Bandler.

The two theorized that the brain can learn healthy patterns and behaviors and that this can bring about positive physical and emotional effects. The basic premise of NLP is that the words we use reflect an inner, subconscious perception of our problems. If these words and perceptions are inaccurate, they will create an underlying problem as long as we continue to use and to think them. (The converse is to change your thoughts to achieve a healthy behavior.)

Reflection

There will be challenges and barriers in your life. In all of our lives! Use your tools to overcome pre-programmed tapes and the Gremlin's force. Change the conscious words you say to yourselves to empowering ones. Know that you can control areas of your life by controlling and/or changing your thoughts. Believe it! The concept of changing the way you think is a powerful tool to change your perspective. Changing perspective allows you to view a situation in a different way, it opens possibilities and allows you to choose what aspect of a situation on which you wish to focus. The situation has not changed; your perspective and response have. Remember the kaleidoscope, the pieces are the same, yet with a twist, the picture is totally different. Also changing how you respond to Gremlin pre-programmed tapes and using empowering language gives you a new perspective. "F.L.I.P. It," your tool for changing your conscious thoughts.

6

Bring Your "A" Game: 100% Living

Tools to Live at 100%

You have heard the motto "Be the best you can be." The Army had a point. Think about you at your best! The previous chapters are guides to being and doing your best, and overcoming barriers. This one will give you direction on how to live at 100%. Add the following ideas to those you already know and do.

Life is not about how fast you run or how high you climb, but how well you bounce. Vivian Komori

It is not the years in your life but the life in your years that counts. Adlai Stevenson

There are only two ways to live your life. One is as though nothing is a miracle. The other is as though everything is a miracle. Albert Einstein

Life is a daring adventure or nothing at all. Helen Keller

Life is what we make it, always has been, always will be. Grandma Moses

You have the choice of how you choose to live, how you show up in the world. Your choice has a strong impact on you and those you interact with. Think about what your life would look like if you were living at 100%? What are some of the ways you believe will contribute to it? Take a minute to see the vision.

_____

_____

_____

_____

_____

_____

Living at 100% brings into account not only who you are *being;* important as well is what you are *doing*—the behaviors and actions you exhibit, the things you do and the things you don't do. Adding to the ideas you have about living at 100% are the following.

Creating Desired Habits

Bad habits are easily developed. You can also develop good ones. Here is one way to start. List up to ten or more routine habits you have now. Examples may include:

I wash dishes daily, file paperwork weekly, drink 8 glasses of water daily, have weekly fun night with the family, clean my work desk at the end of the day, run 4 times a week, go to church regularly, get to work early, am kind to the elderly, volunteer weekly, etc.

Now write *your* habits, the ones you think are both major and minor.

Habits I Have Now	

Look at your "current" habit list, the things you take for granted, the things you do as a matter of course. (There are people who wish they did what you take for granted. Heck, I wish I was one of those people who could get out of bed when the alarm first rings, or who sorts and organizes their bills as they come in the mail.)

What values show up in the things you currently do?

Example 1. Say you put away whatever is lying around in the house before you go to bed—your shoes, the dishes in the drain board, books on tables, etc. You are exhibiting values of cleanliness, order, and organization.

Example 2. I have a friend who always calls to check on me as she does for all of her family. Her values are being loving, caring, and family-oriented.

Example 3. For me, cleaning and organizing my closet is something I always do. It lines up with my values of order, cleanliness, freedom (to be able to find what I want) and it is fun.

Go back to your current habit list and for each of your current habits, note a value next to each item. (See the list in the appendix for ideas.)

Why? How can the identification of values and attributes help? Remember my desire to do paperwork as it arrives? I thought about how the feeling of *freedom* to find what I needed was important to me. I considered how being *orderly* in this area would be. (Two of my values). I knew I would have peace of mind in the orderliness. The more I looked at it this way (rather than as a dreaded task) made it easier to *want* to do something different. I decided to set an Intention to make it easier.

> The "So That" tool in use..... So that I could feel the lightness and freedom of the completed task, and that I was in control of the ever present paperwork, I will take baby steps each day to minimize and organize it. My action steps were to brainstorm possibilities, and align my desire with my values, making sure it was strongly anchored.

As I thought about different possibilities, I came up with an idea that would work. I did it. I got a huge accordion file and threw stuff in it as it came. Seems so easy but previously for me it wasn't. Looking at it in another way, I used the power of one of my (previously identified) basic attributes, aligned my desires with it, got a new perspective and everything was different. Although not perfect, I began to break the habit of a lifetime. You can do it as well.

The curious thing is we always focus on and give our energy to the habits that are desired, the things that are yet to be done. Refer back to your current habits list. It is important to look at the many habits we do have and see what makes them easy for us.

Now list new habits you want!

Remember, these are habits you believe will add to your life. For example, making the bed every morning would not be a good choice if you don't care if it only gets made when you change sheets.

Habits I Want to Have	
1.	
2.	
3.	
4.	
5.	
6.	
7.	
8.	
9.	
10.	

Refer back to your list of current habits. Look at the values you assigned to each. (Go back to chapter one and refer back to your core values.) Take one or two to start, and note a value the desired habit aligns with. Use the strength of that value, which is part of who you are, to change your perspective about the desire. Set an Intention, and use the power of your values to empower the change. Brainstorm possibilities and choose one that you want to do. See how developing your desired habits becomes more attainable.

Minimize your Timewasters

What kind of energy do you tie up leaving things incomplete? Sometimes the to-do things that we wish to complete weigh on us more than the energy to do them? How can you eliminate those things that waste your time? Here's an idea.

List some things you do that are your time wasters, excuses, etc. For me, cleaning a closet is a way for me to procrastinate. (Remember I like doing it.) It feels productive, but is not when I have a scheduled task to complete. Other times I read one of my "just for entertainment" books for just a minute, when I have committed to be productive on a project.

What are some of the things you do to procrastinate?

_____

_____

_____

_____

_____

Be able to identify quickly when you are going into procrastination mode. I know when I start to organize my dresser drawers, I am procrastinating. Yes it may have gotten just a little messy. But I would have to admit that it is not as important as a time-sensitive deadline. That awareness is the first step to making a different choice.

Tackle the To-Do List

I call it the 4 "D's" to getting things done. This is for you if you have a To-Do list that's as long as the U.S. Constitution.

(Guilty as charged. My list often looks like I could work around the clock and never get it completed.) One way to make the list more manageable is to assign each item on the list one of the "Four DDDD's." Look carefully at each item and then decide that you will:

Do it – It is important, you want to do it so make it happen!

Date it – You want to do it but it is not a priority, you can truly do it after the priority tasks. Assign a date when you will consider your next step with the item. Don't do anything about it until then. Don't even think about it.

Delegate it – You do not have to do everything yourself; sometimes there are others who could help. Some things are even better done by others with more time and inclination.

Dump it – That's right, it has been on the To-Do list for so long that it has cobwebs. You have not done it because it is not really important. Or you just do not want to do it. Dump it. Take it off of the list.

Get Past Procrastination

You have pared down the list to those that are on the Do-It list (Or your action steps from chapter 4). What would it take to just do the task? You can make it a bit simpler.

- Think about what it would take to complete your task.

- Break it down into individual manageable tasks.

- Pick a time to work.

- Pick a place.

• Get your materials together.

• Make a first step to just do it (or just do something) and you are on your way.

The following are other components to living your "A" Game, keys to being your best self.

Factors in Living Your "A" Game
Acknowledge

Acknowledge all things and in all ways. You just finished a major to-do item. It is crucially important to acknowledge what you have accomplished, both large and small successes. Don't just go on to the next item on the list. Much like climbing a ladder, each success is a rung up the ladder and without the acknowledgement, it is as if you did something, stepped down off the ladder and started again on another ladder. Instead, let each accomplishment be a step up, taking you closer to your pinnacle.

Celebrate

Acknowledging and celebrating success is another key component to being where (and how) you want to be. You can't pat yourself on the back too often to celebrate your successes. Remember the Law of Attraction: your goal is to get positive energy flowing out and back into you. Good attracts more good. Celebrations are positive energy in abundance.

Practice Gratitude

Gratefulness is an important component to building your

ongoing "ladder to success." Be grateful in all things. Think of a child who you give gifts to, gifts that are both heartfelt and loving. And this child never says much besides a cursory thank you. And then think of the child who is so appreciative, so grateful, and joyful for even small gifts. Which do you most enjoy giving gifts to? It is the same in life. Life will give you more of what you are being and more of what you are contributing. Be grateful.

Keep a Positive Attitude

Attitude is another important "A" Game attribute. Attitude is defined as "a position as indicating action, feeling, or mood; it is the way a person views something or tends to behave towards it, often in an evaluative way."

People often look at their lives in terms of where they came from and what they lack. But it's not the facts of one's environment but your *attitude* toward it that determines if you win or lose, are defeated or victorious. Your attitude is more important than your past, your education, your money, circumstances, failures and successes. It is more important than what other people think, say or do. Attitude is more important than appearance, giftedness or skill. You have a choice everyday regarding the attitude you will embrace for that day. You cannot change your past, you cannot change the fact that people will act in a certain way. You cannot change the world around you. The only thing you can do is play the hand you have been dealt, and that is by choosing your attitude. Life is 10% what happens and 90% of how we react to it. We are in charge of our attitudes.

You cannot control what happens to you, but you can control your attitude toward what happens to you, and in that, you will be mastering change rather than allowing it to master you. Brian Tracy

I could complain about not having certain advantages in my childhood, and I could decide it gives me the right to have a poor attitude. The true fact is others have had less, have had physical limitations and have not used their situation as an excuse. None of those circumstances seals in concrete the person you are to become and how you approach your world.

Your attitude, (your thoughts) about anything will either empower or disempower you. You can choose to dwell on past negatives of your life, and feel that the world has handed you a bad hand, and you deserve to be unhappy. Or, you can declare the "Statute of Limitations" has run out. What is past is past. The future is dependent on what you choose to think about it. Attitude is a choice. In others word: Choose. Decide! What powers your attitude? Your past or your choice? Where you go tomorrow is in part dependent on what your attitude is today.

Be A Contributor

Remember the Law of Attraction and how abundance works: give it away to receive it. Our role in this life has different components. I believe one is to contribute to others. Here are examples of contribution impacts great and small, and what I learned.

I was talking to friend, a tax preparation volunteer, who spoke about a person he knew who contributed what he thought was a really great thing. He thought what the other person was doing was something valuable. What he did not think about nor realize was that what he was doing was a great (although seemingly small to him) contribution to people who needed tax help and could not afford services as expert as his. He was a retired IRS agent who volunteered five hours each Saturday from January to April 15 to help people. I said to him his impact was greater than he could have imagined; he had impacted many lives over the twelve years or more he had been volunteering his time. And yes, I was happy to be able to tell him of his impact and thank him for being who he was.

There was a time that I shattered bones in my foot and could not walk for half a year. I was on one of those "oh-so attractive, impossible to maintain dignity "scooters. One of my greatest challenges, my deepest dread, was that my then two-year-old German shepherd needed to go for walks and I could do nothing. Then a miracle happened. A friend mentioned my dilemma to a person she knew. This woman who I had never met before offered to walk my dog. She did so for months, both rain or shine. She thought that it was no big thing, she needed the exercise anyway. I had the pleasure to tell her that she was a gift. Not only did she take care of my beloved puppy, she showed me kindness and generosity by being such a loving, caring person. What an example to me. Since then, I try to be more like her. Her act of contribution to my life was truly life-changing for me. She made me better.

Look For The Gift (Silver lining)

Many times life seems to kick you in the teeth. It may not be easy but each time you can decide to search for the gift. A while back, I got a clear look at how life can turn on a dime. The idiom describes a life that has a change that comes quickly and dramatically. A number of years ago I sold my home of 24 years to move into my current home. I took a week of vacation to move in and get settled. I returned to work that following Monday and was laid off that Thursday. However (not my first thought as you can imagine), I did think of this as a test of who I was.

Life is determined by how you choose to react or respond, and by how you choose to think. I had a choice of how I could view and react to the circumstances. I was not immediately OK with the situation. I did think it was not the worst that could happen (a saying my daughter and I had). I decided to change my perspective and look at the gift. My gift was that the layoff did not happen between the time I sold my old home and when my new home closed, jeopardizing the close of the new home.

It was July first, the height of summer and I decided to have the "Summer of My Life!" I spent the summer on my deck entertaining and playing. Sometimes getting up early in the morning, making coffee and just sitting outside listening to the morning. The summer was excellent. I definitely "made lemonade."

Fast forward. After some months, I had several temporary positions, but not the permanent job I wanted. I was unsure about what would happen, but I decided to trust the process and have faith. At times it was highly frustrating, but what I did was to make a "job" of job hunting: up every morning at 8:00 to do the daily tasks I assigned for myself. I believed in the best, I had faith, and I took action.

The dime turned again. My long and hard job search finally paid off. I got a job I would have killed for, with excellent opportunities to do the things I loved to do. It was a position I would not have had if I had not been laid off.

Two things to remember.

1. Whatever life throws you, you have a choice in how you respond.

2. That dark clouds could have a platinum lining.

10,000 Mistakes

Contrary to the belief of the perfectionist, no one is perfect. Everyone makes mistakes. The thing is to not let the mistakes define you. Or let the weight of them drag you down. I had a client who would beat herself up when she made mistakes, or did not do things she thought she should. Little mistakes or big ones were cause to see herself as lacking. It could have been spilling marinara sauce while out to dinner, forgetting a date, turning a work project in late, or burning dinner. The list could go on and on. Then I asked her what would happen if she would allow herself at least 10,000 mistakes, (and another 10,000 if she used them up). She said the ability to allow herself mistakes was freeing. The lesson is: don't beat yourself up by focusing on what you do wrong now or did wrong in the past. Allow yourself the mistake. Let it go. Look only to what you will do differently if you need to.

Good Communication

Living at 100% affects your interaction with others. The level of integrity that you show others is dependent on good communication. It could be your friend, your teacher, your children, your boss, your mate or anyone else.

> *I know that you believe you understand what you think I said, but I'm not sure you realize that what you heard is not what I meant.* Robert McCloskey

To be your best with others, all communications should be:

Clear

Direct

Honest

Honoring

Clear. Sometimes we expect others to intuit or guess what we mean. Men say it makes them crazy when women are exhibiting anger, but will not say why. Note, this is not true for just women! BE CLEAR. Being clear is also asking for what you want. For example: Do not say I wish you would help more around the house; clearly ask to "please have the garbage emptied after dinner" or "please read to the children tonight".

Direct. Say exactly what you mean. Do not make the responsibility of knowing what you are thinking someone else's. Don't allude to, beat around the bush or speak in parables. How many times do you read that people will say you should know why I am angry? Instead of just saying they are angry. Be direct!

Honest. What needs to be said here? Honesty is still the best policy.

Honoring. This is sometimes difficult. How do you speak to others in a way that they feel honored? Sometimes honoring means listening carefully and hearing what they are saying. Letting them know they are being heard is honoring. Sometimes it could be in a tense situation and you want to say something difficult, but want to say it in a way the other person will hear, accept *and not feel attacked.* For example, in a disagreement with someone, use "I" statements. "I felt hurt, and not respected." Not, "You made me feel…" Instead of saying, "You never make time for me," try saying "I need more quality time to spend with you." The use of the word "You" puts others in the state of self-protection, it can make them feel compelled to attack back. Honoring conversation is speaking to others as you would wish to be spoken to, in a way they hear you but still feel no threat, no condemnation, truly feel honored while you say what you want and need.

Here is an opportunity to visualize your future into existence. Take a moment, think about the visioning exercises you did and see a vision with you at 100%, you at the top of your game.

What does it feel like? It might be that you feel you are free and flying, that you have been given the Holy Grail, that you can do all things, be all things. It may feel powerful. What do you think it would feel like to you?

_____

_____

_____

_____

_____

Another way to build on this concept is to think about you at the culmination of your vision. Now give yourself an "A" for how fantastic you were, how you "rocked" that accomplishment. Now, what did you do to get the A? Were you bold and fearless? Were you committed? Did you put all your Intentions and attention on the vision, and work toward it? Did you keep the faith, stayed encouraged, give and receive help, do the mundane with a smile, etc. Think about all the things you did over the period of time for which you deserved an "A." Write what you did to get the A.

_____

_____

_____

_____

_____

Reflection

These are some of the ways that you can be at the top of your game, living at 100%. Just remember, as you walk through life, you can be the person who makes a positive impact and provides a legacy for others.

7

Take Care of You

What is the most important thing you can do for yourself, take care of yourself. It is impossible to truly thrive without the foundational block of self-care. With self-care you are better able to exercise positive choices and overcome challenges.

Sometimes the most important thing in a whole day is the rest we take between two deep breaths. Etty Hillesum

Don't take life too seriously. You'll never get out of it alive. Elbert Hubbard

One of the secrets of a happy life is continuous small treats. Iris Murdoc

When you recover or discover something that nourishes your soul and brings joy, care enough about yourself to make room for it in your life. Jean Shinoda Bolen

Declare today "sacred time"—off-limits to everyone, unless invited by you. Take care of your personal wants and needs. Say no, graciously but firmly, to others' demands. Oprah Winfrey

Enjoy life – there are no re-runs. Shirley Lowery

It is often easy to focus on what will get us to our vision, to be more of what we wish to become, to do more of what we want to do, to accomplish more. If you think of all the previous chapters as foundational blocks, then this is the cornerstone. Unless you take care of yourself, nothing else matters. It's not always easy and we must sometimes (many times) remind ourselves. The next example is about a discovery I made about "Kairos" and letting yourself go.

Kairos: Sometimes taking care of self just means to let yourself go. Much of my life consists of planning my time and working with clients, developing my business, writing a book, my ongoing quest for learning, my (spectacular, lovable, super intelligent, sweet natured) dog, training him as a working dog, (he's certified by Therapy Dogs International as a "Tail Waggin' Tutor"), daily walks for and with him, German Shepherd Club meetings, book club meetings, kickboxing, church, reading, errands, chores, and, oh yeah, coaching high school youth, Pilates, and Zumba. Although I do not do everything all the time the list still seems to go on and on.

One time I found myself unable to relax and just do nothing… and I was on vacation. I had just returned from a trip to the ocean and was to leave for the San Francisco Bay area in two days. I was watching TV but was not enjoying it because I felt tremendous guilt as I thought that I:

Should be working on my to-do list items,

Could be doing chores,

Ought to be running errands,

Need to....

I found it impossible to just <u>NOT Do Anything</u> unless I felt it was "productive." I had a hard time just sitting around and reading a book or watching TV without feelings of guilt. (Recovering over-achieving Type A personality.)

What is it about many of us that make us think every moment must be task oriented? I thought, what I wanted, what I needed, was to be able to allow myself, (give myself permission) to *not be productive*. What I really wanted was to not have to do that which I thought I <u>SHOULD</u> do. I made a decision that I could do nothing if I wanted to. It was as if a beacon of light shined on the idea. WOW! I could have time in which I did NOT have to do a "should" and I did NOT have to feel guilty. I determined that I deserved it and even more, that it was necessary. So I instituted a "no-should" time.

Kairos

I wanted to anchor the idea. It needed a name (totem/image) that exemplified the concept. And I wanted a term that was more empowering than "no should time." When trying to decide what to call it, I found the word Kairos. I really like this.

Kairos (καιρός) is an ancient Greek word meaning the right or opportune moment (supreme moment). The ancient Greeks had two words for time, *chronos* and *kairos*. While the former refers to *chronological* or sequential time, the latter signifies a *time in between*, a moment of undetermined period of time in which something special happens. What the special something is depends on who is using the word. While chronos is quantitative, kairos has a qualitative nature. According to ancient Greeks, Kairos was the god of the fleeting moment, a favorable opportunity opposing the fate of man. Such a moment must be grasped; otherwise the moment is gone and cannot be re-captured.

Eureka, (and that is not a word typically I use, but it fit the moment). It was the feeling I wanted. Chronos is the time of responsibility, the time for doing the things that I defined as productive. Kairos time is a time of choice. A time where I am free. A time where there is creativity, peace, and freedom. It is tranquil and serene. It is the time between work and responsibility. It is the place where I am renewed. Time and space are open. The time NOT spent on to-do items where "shoulds" do not have power. It's the time where something special happens. I am attuned to what I am doing and experiencing—time flies, my mind is open and free. Unlike a void in space, it is a time filled with possibilities. My Kairos time.

So really, what I found is that down time is not unproductive time, it could actually be the most productive time of all. Kairos time is focusing on and losing oneself in something, anything. I can get the experience from reading, walking, working on art projects, Pilates, kick boxing, watching TV, talking on the phone to a close friend, staring at the ocean, or just doing "nothing." Other ways to have Kairos may be with meditation, massage, yoga. I have mine, you choose yours. Claim Kairos. This is a prime way to take care of yourself. It is freeing, energizing, balancing and restoring.

Take Time for You

You can't always control the circumstances that life throws your way, but you can control how well you take care of yourself. Taking proper care of your body, soul and mind can keep you in optimum mental health and ready for life's challenges. And while it's sometimes hard to decide whether to take the down time when you face so many other priorities, taking care of yourself is just as important as any other priority. Self-care is necessary for a balanced life.

How do we justify taking time out for a workout or a healthy lunch or an art class when our to-do lists are a mile long? This question gets at our mindset about taking the time for these things. If you want to make successful and lasting progress toward your goals this year, prioritizing self is a critical shift in mindset that you MUST make.

What is your mindset about me-time and self-care? The very busy president of the United States (and every past president) makes time in his unbelievably hectic life for regular exercise (as well as for leisure and other self-care). Does that tell you something about how important and life-enhancing caring for yourself is? And how even with a busy schedule it can be done?

Consider the costs of NOT taking the time you need for yourself. This includes NOT taking the time you need to move forward on your important goals. Consequences of not getting enough of what you need to thrive include:

- Declining health and wellness.

- Reduced productivity.

- Diminished focus (including getting distracted from your own goals and priorities).

- Exhaustion.

- Stress and burnout.

When we take time for ourselves and contribute to ourselves:

We have more zest and energy for our desired responsibilities.

We see ourselves, our ideas and visions as valuable.

We play bigger, think broader and are more successful.

We have more energy, focus, and clarity.

We are more confident.

We have greater access to our dreams and goals.

Taking time out to care for yourself can remind you and others that you and your needs are important. Try it.

Challenge Yourself

Sound good? Here's your challenge:

What do you need to do to claim the time or energy that you require this week?

What do you need to let go of or say no to in order for that to happen?

What one action can you take to be more committed to your self-care goals this week?

What will you do to take care of YOU?

Things You Have Heard (Ignored) Before
Here are a few ideas and suggestions. Add your own to this list.

Get Enough Sleep.

Take up healthy eating habits.

Exercise regularly.

(I cannot say enough about the three above.)

Read a book just for fun.

Take a bubble bath.

Find a hobby.

Pamper yourself.

Garden.

Sing loudly.

Go shoe shopping (or is that just my thing?).

Do breathing exercises.

Start a journal.

Laugh, especially at yourself.

Relax.

Say no.

Drink plenty of water.

Practice meditation or yoga.

Pray.

Play more games.

Take time to be in stillness.

Smile more.

Call your family often.

Dream more while you are awake.

Try to make at least three people smile each day.

Clean and de-clutter.

Get rid of anything that isn't useful, beautiful or joyful.

Do something good for others.

Invest your energy in the present moment.

Be still.

Don't overdo. Keep your limits.

Don't waste your precious energy on gossip.

Forget issues of the past.

Make peace with your past so it won't spoil the present.

Know that no one is in charge of your happiness except you.

Forgive everyone for everything.

However good or bad a situation is, know it will change.

No matter how you feel, get up, dress up and show up.

Practice gratitude always.

Practice being a positive, encouraging person.

Maintain social support.

Process your emotions.

Have the right attitude.

Keep your mind sharp.

Maintain a spiritual practice.

Have quiet time.

Be a friend.

Clear distractions to be more present.

Play.

Lastly, bring it back to you. The coaching questions would be:

> How can a focus on self-care serve you?

> What can you do to make it a priority?

> What will you do?

Don't Take Yourself So Seriously

Taking a mental or emotional vacation allows you to come back to the reality of your life feeling refreshed and relaxed. Sometimes you should just do something crazy and fun, something that's outside your normal self. Sometimes you need to not take everything so seriously. **Remember that tasks are not all of what life is all about.** One of my mottos in life is having an "endless supply of moments that take my breath away." (I read that somewhere and it stuck.)

So..... If your life starts to get out of hand, you could do what I do: **Play!**

What simple things on this list might make you happy?

Sing into your hairbrush.

Dance.

Play a game where you make up the rules as you go along.

Find some pretty stones and save them.

Eat dessert first.

Laugh out loud.

Give yourself a gold star for everything you do today.

Call a friend and ask the person to come out and play.

In bare feet, walk along the surf at the beach.

Make snow angels.

Lie on the grass at night and look at the stars.

Visit a zoo.

Watch a Disney movie.

Go to Disneyland.

Etc., Etc., Etc.

Do anything that makes you smile and brings you joy. To make sure you have a list of things to pull out of your toy box when you need to "Go Play." you may want to make a list of 10 simple things that make you happy. Remember, knowledge is power.

_____

_____

_____

_____

_____

_____

Reflection

Kairos, the time where something special happens is a choice. Cronos, the time I call productive reality time will always be there. It may be work, caring for your family, or the many errands of everyday life. You can't escape it. Just keep the two in balance so that you .... Take care of you!

Final Reflection/Reminders

In this guidebook to getting out of your own way, I trust you have learned new concepts, (or been reminded of ones you already know).

- You have clearly defined who you are and that knowledge gives you personal power.
- Your over-riding values have been identified and will serve as a filter for all you do.
- You have created both short-term and long-term visions for your life, some very detailed, and others broad but Intentional. In fact, you have learned the power of an Intention which serves to draw you toward it with clearly understood underlying motivations.
- The challenging task of overcoming barriers is better understood with tools to change your perspective and response. You know that you have the power to change your mind.
- You have been given ideas on how to live your best life.
- You know there is power in balancing your busy life with downtime, to take care of yourself.

Everything you have read depends on you making choices. Choose what works for you. Choose to do different things to increase satisfaction in your life. Choose to implement the presented concepts.

This book is not about changing who you are. It is a guide-book to help you choose to change aspects of your life to make it the best possible. So you will…..

Get out of your own way and design an extraordinary life.

About The Author

Patricia Knight is an International Coach Federation certified, accredited Life Coach, a speaker, trainer and program consultant. She specializes in working with high-performing individuals committed to living true to their values while discovering new possibilities to greater levels of success, (There are also those who desire to do so.) She has worked with leaders from Fortune 500 companies including Microsoft, Boeing, government leaders, entrepreneurial owners and athletes. She also speaks to and implements leadership programs for youth. She has a degree in Psychology and Math and is founder of Kaleidoscope Life Coaching, motivating and inspiring clients to success since 2006. Her eclectic career includes counseling, case management, marketing, training, strategic planning and project development.

She lives in the beautiful northwest city of Seattle, Washington with the world's smartest German Shepherd. To renew and keep balanced, she travels, spends time with her family and friends, does Zumba and Pilates, takes long walks with her dog, draws, and reads.

For questions or comments.

Visit www.Kaleidocoach.com or email Patricia@Kaleidocoach.com.

Resources

Invite Change (formerly Academy for Coach Training) is the International Coaching Federation accredited training program where I received my certification. It is located in Edmunds Washington. Some of the concepts presented were covered in the course of training: The Values (list of words) Exercise and Single Daily Action (S.D.A.). Also covered were the Gremlin, and the Wheel of Life. Other authors' also present versions of those ideas.

The Gremlin

Laura Whitworth, Karen Kimsey-House and Henry Kimsey-House, Co-Active Coaching

Rick Carson, Taming Your Gremlin

Ryan Godsell, The Saboteur

Matt Hudson, The Saboteur Within

Kate Collins-Donnelly, Starving the Anger Gremlin

The Wheel of Life

Laura Whitworth, Karen and Henry Kimsey-House, Co-Active Coaching

Pam Richardson, The Life Coach

Values Exercise

Laura Whitworth, Karen Kimsey-House and Henry Kimsey-House, Co-Active Coaching

Made in the USA
San Bernardino, CA
02 October 2015